SOUTH AFRICAN FOLK SONGS
COLLECTION

ARRANGED BY

JAMES WILDING &
NKULULEKO ZUNGU

ISBN 978-1-70514-173-1

Visit Hal Leonard Online at
www.halleonard.com

World headquarters, contact:
Hal Leonard
7777 West Bluemound Road
Milwaukee, WI 53213
Email: info@halleonard.com

In Europe, contact:
Hal Leonard Europe Limited
42 Wigmore Street
Marylebone, London, W1U 2RN
Email: info@halleonardeurope.com

In Australia, contact:
Hal Leonard Australia Pty. Ltd.
4 Lentara Court
Cheltenham, Victoria, 3192 Australia
Email: info@halleonard.com.au

From the Arrangers

We come from the beautiful country of South Africa.

South Africa evolved from a land of racial injustice to one of democratic inclusion through the first democratic elections in 1994. The elections led to our country's first Black president, Nelson Mandela, often called the "Father of the Nation" (Tat' uMadiba in isiXhosa). He and many other significant freedom fighters shared a vision for a country, a vision of different cultures living together in acceptance and love:

> "Each of us is intimately attached to the soil of this beautiful country... a rainbow nation at peace with itself and the world."

New formats of unity and inclusion have created an environment where people once forced to live apart (i.e. Apartheid) can now live together. During Apartheid the music of South Africa's various cultures and racial groups developed separately. It is long overdue to bring these contrasting musical traditions together in one anthology that reflects all the cultures of our diverse nation.

In this collection, we share pieces inspired by music traditions of many different South African cultural groups including Afrikaans, AmaNdebele, AmaXhosa, AmaZulu, BaPedi, BaSotho, BaTswana, Cape Malay, EmaSwati, and Vatsonga.

We would like to acknowledge the countless friends and relatives who have contributed with suggestions, practical advice, and lists of favorite folk songs. A big thank you to the musicians whose performances on Hugh Tracey's mid-20th c. "Sound of Africa" project inspired some of these arrangements. Our special gratitude goes to Charmaine Siagian, our tireless editor for this wonderful project, who taught us little things along the way; for example, that our Afrikaans word for banana (*piesang*) comes from the Malay word *pisang*.

About the Arrangers

James Wilding is of British heritage and was born and raised in South Africa. He studied at the University of Cape Town, and later moved to the United States to continue his studies at Youngstown State University and Kent State University. He has received commissions from Bayerischer Rundfunk, the South African Music Rights Organization, the Tuesday Musical Association, and the Orange County School of the Arts; and his music has been prescribed for the UNISA-Transnet International Piano Competition. Dr. Wilding teaches composition and theory at The University of Akron in Ohio.

South African-born composer **Nkululeko Zungu** is a graduate of the University of Northern Colorado where his studies focused on contemporary composition. He finds pleasure in exploring music from traditional Classical to modern Electronic. His music has been performed by the Wet Ink Ensemble as well as in performance spaces at the University of Cape Town, UCLA, and the Fort Collins Museum of Discovery. Nkululeko has taught piano for several years in both Cape Town and Colorado, and recently presented a lecture on South African music at Hong Kong Adventist College. He places much importance on sharing his culture through his writing and pedagogy.

TABLE OF CONTENTS

4 NOTES ON THE FOLK SONGS

8 THEY SAY THERE'S A MAN IN THE MOON
HULLE SÊ DAAR'S 'N MAN IN DIE MAAN

10 MOM DID NOT WRITE THIS LETTER!
ASINGOMAMA LOBEBHALA LENCWADI

12 SARIE MARAIS

14 I HAVE A SWEETHEART IN DURBAN
NDINESIPONONO SAM ETHEKWINI

16 MAMA, WHO IS THIS?
MAMA NGUBANI NA LO?

18 JAN PIEREWIET

21 THE AXE CUTS THE THORN TREE
SELEPE GA SE A JA MOSU

23 WHAT HAVE WE DONE?
SENZENI NA?

24 HOPE, DON'T LEAVE ME
THEMBEKILE

26 DELILAH, MY WIFE, SEE MY STRENGTH
SAMSON NODELILAH

28 THE DOVES ABOVE
NALO NALO NALO IHOBE

30 HERE COMES THE ALIBAMA
DAAR KOM DIE ALIBAMA

32 OUR DEAREST MOTHERS
OOMAMA BETHU, ESIBATHANDAYO

34 SUGAR BUSH
SUIKERBOSSIE

36 I AM IN CHARGE, IT WILL BE KNOWN
KUZAKWAZIWANA

38 GO FORWARD
SHOSHOLOZA

41 THE DAY WE POUND EARTH
MOTLA RE TULANG MOBU

44 THE CLOUDS, THEY THUNDER
KWAKHUPHUKA AMAFU DALI, LEZA LADUMA LAMTHATA

46 THE CROWING OF THE ROOSTER
IQHUDE WEMA, LAKHALA KABINI KATHATHU

48 COME OUT OF YOUR CAVE, NCOFULA
INCABA NO NCOFULA

50 HEY, THERE THEY ARE
HEE KE BALE

52 DANCE
MASESA

NATIONAL ANTHEMS | PATRIOTIC

55 LAND OF OUR FATHERS
FATSHE LA BONTATA RONA

59 GOD BLESS AFRICA
NKOSI SIKELEL' IAFRIKA

62 GUIDE TO CULTURAL GROUPS, LANGUAGES, AND TRADITIONS

63 MAP OF SOUTH AFRICA AND LESOTHO

NOTES ON THE FOLK SONGS

THEY SAY THERE'S A MAN IN THE MOON |
HULLE SÊ DAAR'S 'N MAN IN DIE MAAN (page 8)

I didn't know this tender lullaby until I started gathering ideas for this collection. An Afrikaans friend said it was her childhood favorite, and I immediately fell in love with it. Play as softly as you can. -JW

MOM DID NOT WRITE THIS LETTER! |
ASINGOMAMA LOBEBHALA LENCWADI (page 10)

This isiXhosa song is sung by those who live far from home. The lyrics describe a young child receiving a letter from home, but they recognize that the letter is not truly from their mother because their mother would surely have begun with: "My *dearest* child..." The boisterous rhythm provides the character of the piece and depicts the determination of the child. -NZ

SARIE MARAIS (page 12)

The melody for this Afrikaans song is taken from "Sweet Ellie Rhee," written by American Septimus Winner in 1865, and its meaning, the loss of a loved one during wartime, was translated roughly from the US Civil War to the South African War.[1] There is one slight difference: where the US version is "Sweet Ellie Rhee, so dear to me, is lost forever more," the Afrikaners have the more optimistic "*My Sarie Marais is so ver van my hart, Maar'k hoop om haar weer te sien (My Sarie Marais is so far from my heart, but I hope to see her again)*." -JW

I HAVE A SWEETHEART IN DURBAN |
NDINESIPONONO SAM ETHEKWINI (page 14)

This vibrant isiXhosa song depicts those in love. "Isiponono" is a nickname given to the one you love (like "sweetheart" or "honey"). Many school choirs during the Apartheid era would perform this song at various social gatherings. As is common in African choirs, singers create their own stylistic dances to depict the joy of the lyrics. Feel free to depict your own enjoyment of the piece! Be sure to create a clear distinction between the call: "*Ndinesiponono*" (the phrase beginning from the upbeat to measure 1) and the response: "*Sam eThekwini*" (the phrase beginning from the upbeat to measure 2). -NZ

MAMA, WHO IS THIS? | *MAMA NGUBANI NA LO?* (page 16)

In Southern Africa, many songs use the call and response technique. After dinner, or any gathering, families often entertain themselves with call and response singing, always creating an environment of pleasure and joy. This isiXhosa song is a conversation between a mother and her young child. As a man approaches, the child asks, "Who is this and what is he bringing us? Could it be a red bottle of amasi?" *Amasi* is fermented milk often drunk with *Umphokoqo* (a crumbed maize meal dish) and is a staple diet in many African households. The name of the meal differs depending on the culture preparing it; for example, the Afrikaans people call it *krummelpap*. -NZ

JAN PIEREWIET (page 18)

This well-known Afrikaans folk song might be as old as the Great Trek.[2] Jan is a man's name (same as John in English) and Pierewiet is an imaginary surname derived from "pirouette" (to turn around on one toe). -JW

---

[1] 1899-1902, also known as the Anglo-Boer War.

[2] Northern migration of Afrikaners starting in the 1830s.

THE AXE CUTS THE THORN TREE | SELEPE GA SE A JA MOSU (page 21)

BaTswana men sing this song when they cut down the mosu thorn tree. The call is "*Serekgo, serekgo!*" (Chop, chop), and the response comes in "*Selepe ga se a ja mosu*" (the axe on the thorn tree). The strong staccato chords in the left hand imitate the axe. -JW

WHAT HAVE WE DONE? | SENZENI NA? (page 23)

"Senzeni na?" is a protest song widely sang during the Apartheid regime. The simple question, "Senzeni na?" (What have we done?) was a cry to anyone who would listen and is still a question that burdens many hearts today. In pre1994 South Africa, the country was under the oppressive laws of Apartheid. These laws sought to benefit white people of European descent and left the Bantu tribes of Southern Africa (Nguni, Southern Nguni, Shangana-Tsonga, Sotho-Tswana, and Venda people) without the ability to develop on equal terms. A profound line from the song, "*Sono sethu, ubumnyama...*" translates: "Our (only) sin is that we are black..." and speaks to the ultimate pain experienced by Black people in the country. -NZ

HOPE, DON'T LEAVE ME | THEMBEKILE (page 24)

"Thembekile" is an isiXhosa song that was commonly sung in Black schools of South African townships in the 1970s. Singing was a social event used to enjoy each other's company. The song introduces us to Thembekile, whose parents and friends are pleading with him not to leave. Often sung by children, it displays a juxtaposition of innocence and guilt, somber and cheer. -NZ

DELILAH, MY WIFE, SEE MY STRENGTH | SAMSON NODELILAH (page 26)

This lighthearted isiXhosa tune tells the Biblical story of Samson and Delilah. Many South Africans who grew up during Apartheid are well versed in Bible stories. These stories were either taught in their Christian households or through the secondary school curriculums of the time that mandated Bible studies. The pedaling in this piece should create a sense of wonder and awe by merging the beautiful melody with the Mixolydian mode. When there is an appoggiatura, the grace note should be played on the beat. -NZ

THE DOVES ABOVE | NALO NALO NALO IHOBE (page 28)

Students in school typically perform this isiXhosa song at school functions such as a music or sporting event. It is sung from the perspective of a child appreciating the beauty of a dove. Many kids who grew up in South African township environments learned the art of turning every observation of life into a musical moment. This song is sung in a sweet and playful way, and the playing of this piece should be the same. When playing the chordal figures, aim for lightness of touch. -NZ

HERE COMES THE ALIBAMA | DAAR KOM DIE ALIBAMA (page 30)

A favorite of the Cape Malay tradition, the origins of this song are obscure. One legend has it that it was customary for young brides to receive a bed made of reeds as a wedding gift. The reeds were transported down river and across the ocean to Cape Town on a ship named the Alibama.[3] People waiting at the harbor are delighted to see the ship arriving. "*Nooi, nooi, die rietkooi, nooi, die rietkooi is gemaak*" (girl, girl, the reed-bed, girl, the reed-bed will be made). When I was a child I couldn't hear the Afrikaans words properly, and unfortunately this part of the song sounded like nonsense to me. -JW

[3] This trade ship Alibama was probably named after the warship CSS Alabama, a confederate navy vessel that raided
Union-friendly ships off Cape Town and other places during the US Civil War.

Our Dearest Mothers | OoMama Bethu, Esibathandayo (page 32)

This isiXhosa song goes, "*OoMama bethu esibathandayo kodwa namhlanje sesibashiyile...*" which translates, "Our dearest Mothers whom we love, today we left them behind..." It's a lament of township life because of kids falling prey to the life of gangsterism thus leaving their mothers alone in their homes. The piece begins in a melancholy way but has moments of hope. This is later juxtaposed by a livelier section depicting gangster life. One line: "*Ootsotsi badlala ama-dice, batshaya instangu, babetha amaphepha, badubula... bahambe!*" translates as, "Gangsters play dice, they smoke marijuana, they play cards, they shoot... and they leave." -NZ

Sugar Bush | Suikerbossie (page 34)

The Sugar Bush (Protea repens) is a shrub of the Western Cape fynbos, with a beautiful large flower. The singer in this Afrikaans song compares the flower to his beloved: "*Suikerbossie, 'k wil jou hê, wat sal jou mamma daarvan sê?*" (Sugar Bush, I want you, what will your mother say about that?) -JW

I Am in Charge, It Will Be Known | Kuzakwaziwana (page 36)

Kuzakwaziwana is an isiZulu song typically sung at competitions as a type of war cry between schools at interschool events. It showed dominance between the various schools. The opening notes - B, G#, B - is a call sung loudly ("Wee-ooo-weee!"). This dominance can also be heard in the lyrics, "*Ndim ophetheyo, ndim intshatsheli*" (I am the one in charge here. I am the champion). A wonderful piece to work on two-against-three playing between the two hands. -NZ

Go Forward | Shosholoza (page 38)

This is South Africa's unofficial second anthem, probably the best-known song in the country. As a boy, I knew the tune from a TV commercial, and naturally assumed it had been invented by that company. But the song was originally sung by AmaNdebele people, who migrated from the north to find work in South Africa. The left hand makes the call "Shosholoza" (go forward), and the right hand gives the response: "*Shosholoza, Kulezo ntaba, stimela siphume South Africa*" (Go forward, from these mountains, on this train to South Africa). -JW

The Day We Pound Earth | Motla Re Tulang Mobu (page 41)

BaPedi women pound their grain with pestle and mortar. They sing of visits from relatives who eat their food without helping with any of the work, and then disappear when there is nothing left to eat. It might be better to pound earth rather than grain for these lazy people: "*Ba xotla ka go kokobetsha ditedu*" (those who come in putting their beards into the food). In the piece, the left hand does the pounding. -JW

The Clouds, They Thunder | Kwakhuphuka Amafu Dali, Leza Laduma Lamthata (page 44)

This energetic isiXhosa song tells the fairytale of Kelinah, who was abducted by a storm. The song is often used as a warmup exercise in music class in Black schools during Apartheid. The character of the piece is energetic, with use of the lower keyboard, as well as accents and contrasting dynamics to convey the thunderous storms. This would be a wonderful piece to showcase at a recital. -NZ

The Crowing of the Rooster | Iqhude weMa, Lakhala Kabini Kathathu (page 46)

In this isiZulu song, we hear someone sing of a rooster that crows in the morning, letting people know that it is time to wake up and fetch water. Many people in villages and some township settings, relied on this animal to be a type of alarm for their morning chores. Interestingly, a song like this was also sung to pass away time while doing those chores. This piece will require focused work on hand independence as the piece uses syncopated rhythms and crossing of hands. Once mastered, this would be another great piece to use on a recital. Please note the performer can ignore all repeat signs if a shorter piece is required, only observing Dal Segno. -NZ

Come Out of Your Cave, Ncofula | Incaba No Ncofula (page 48)

In old times, emaSwati people found shelter and security in caves high up on mountains. In this song, one group tries to lure another into their cave. Be relaxed and free when you play the mysterious tremolos. -JW

Hey, There They Are | Hee Ke Bale (page 50)

BaSotho people discover a strange sight: their cattle have been fighting among each other. The bulls have seriously injured themselves with their horns. The men sing in low tones, while the ladies ululate high above. Play these six boxes in any order but be sure to read the directions above the piece. -JW

Dance | Masesa (page 52)

This is an extremely energetic song used for the Masesa dance of the Vatsonga people. The Vatsonga come from Mozambique, but many have settled in South Africa, often to find work in the gold mines. This takes some practice, but it will be fun to play! -JW

Land of Our Fathers | Fatshe La Bontata Rona (page 55)

The national anthem of Lesotho is included here to pay respect to the world's only country to be completely landlocked by another nation (see map on p. 63). Lesotho is a small mountainous country that relies almost completely on South Africa for its resources. In return, the BaSotho people make a big contribution to the South African labor market. The melody was written by the Swiss composer and teacher Ferdinand Laur as "Freiheit" (Freedom) in 1820. It was repurposed with seSotho words by French missionary François Coillard in the 1860s and became the national anthem of Lesotho in 1967. -JW

God Bless Africa | Nkosi Sikelel' iAfrika (page 59)

The anthem holds enormous value as a prayer for the nation of South Africa. Before the advent of freedom in 1994, the South African president at the time, Frederik Willem de Klerk, preferred that the state have two national anthems: Nkosi Sikelel' iAfrika (written by Enoch Sontonga in 1897) and Die Stem van Suid-Afrika (written by CJ Langenhoven in 1918). After the first democratic elections on April 27, 1994 brought freedom to the country, the first Black president of South Africa, Nelson Rolihlahla Mandela, announced that the national anthem would be a combination of the two existing anthems.

South Africa is a country with 11 official languages. This unique and beautiful cultural variety is captured in the four stanzas of the anthem. The first two stanzas are taken from the hymn Nkosi Sikelel' iAfrika with the first stanza recited in the original isiXhosa and isiZulu languages. The second stanza is the seSotho version of the same hymn, published by Moses Mphahlele in 1942. The third stanza is taken from the hymn "Die Stem van Suid-Afrika" and is recited in Afrikaans. The final stanza is in English and was written by Zaidel-Rudolph. In total, the anthem comprises five of the eleven official languages, making it the only anthem in the world with more than two languages in one national anthem. -NZ

They Say There's a Man in the Moon
(Hulle Sê Daar's 'n Man in die Maan)

South African Folk Song
Arranged by James Wilding

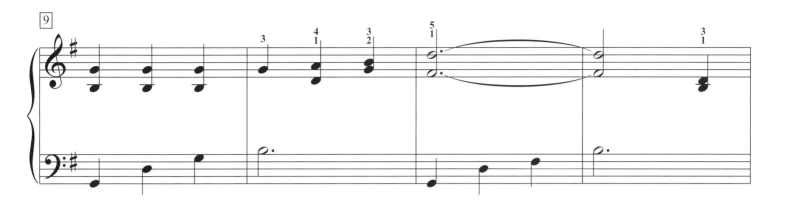

rit. 2nd time

Mom Did NOT Write This Letter!
(Asingomama Lobebhala Lencwadi)

South African Folk Song
Arranged by Nkululeko Zungu

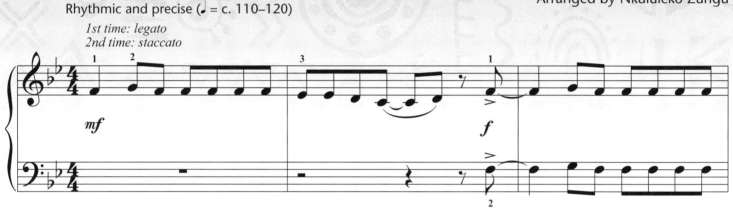

SARIE MARAIS

South African Folk Song
Arranged by James Wilding

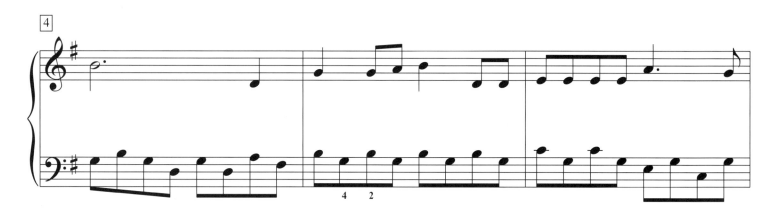

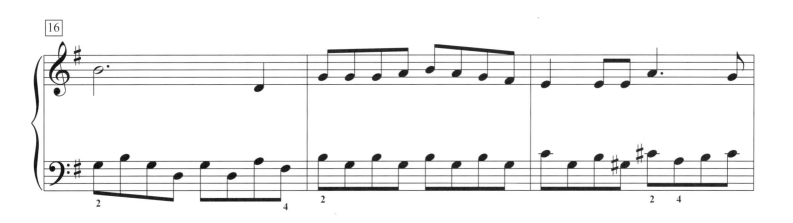

I Have a Sweetheart in Durban
(Ndinesiponono Sam eThekwini)

South African Folk Song
Arranged by Nkululeko Zungu

Joyful call and response (♩ = c. 110–120)

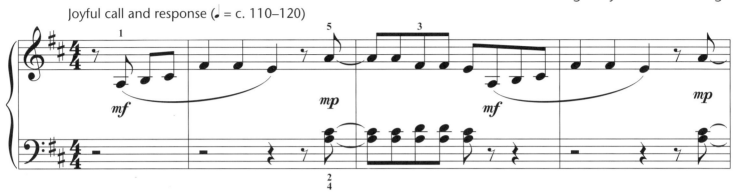

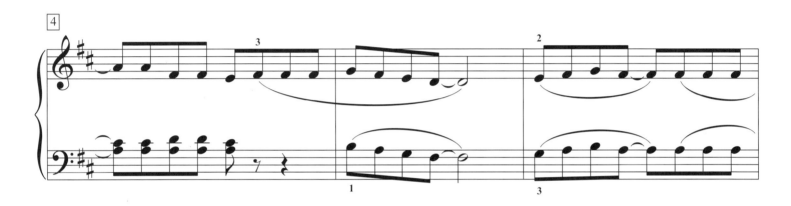

Playful and light

L.H. over R.H.

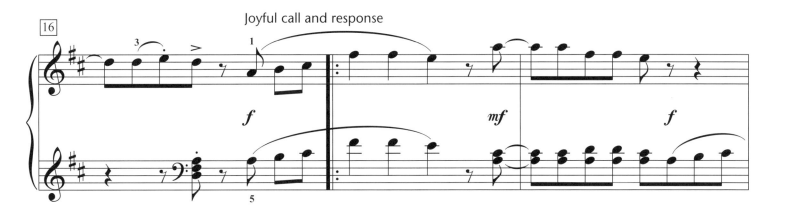

Joyful call and response

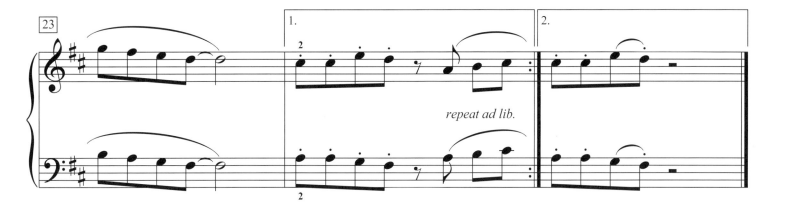

repeat ad lib.

Mama, Who is This?
(Mama, Ngubani Na Lo?)

South African Folk Song
Arranged by Nkululeko Zungu

Moderately (♩ = c. 92–100)

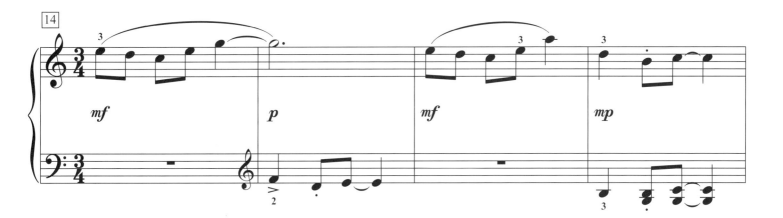

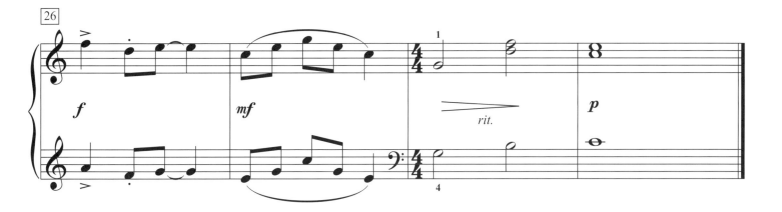

Jan Pierewiet

South African Folk Song
Arranged by James Wilding

Quick and fun (♩ = c. 184)

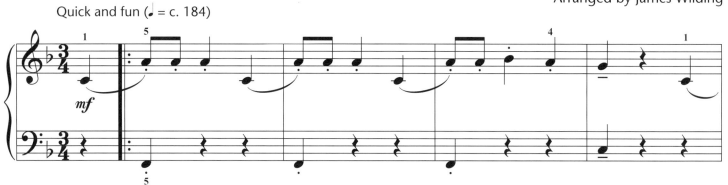

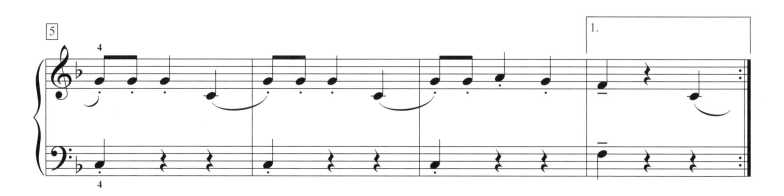

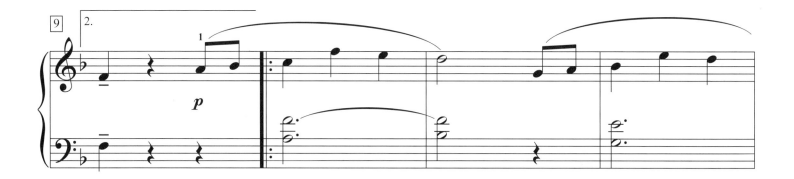

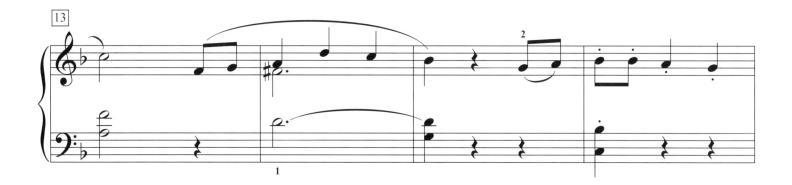

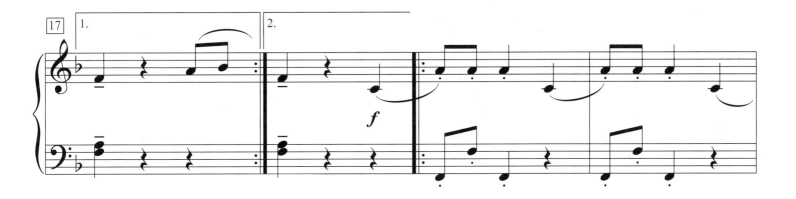

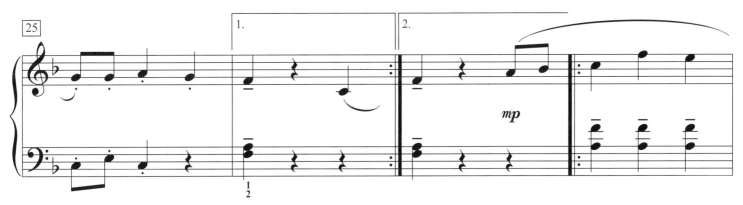

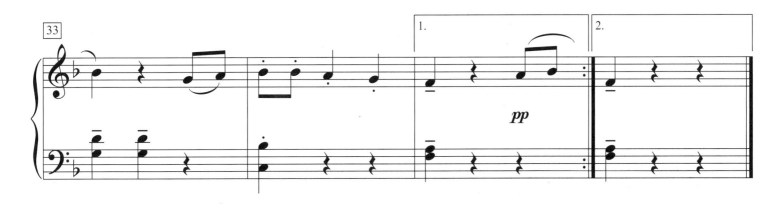

The Axe Cuts the Thorn Tree
(Selepe Ga Se A Ja Mosu)

South African Folk Song
Arranged by James Wilding

Bold (♩ = c. 80)

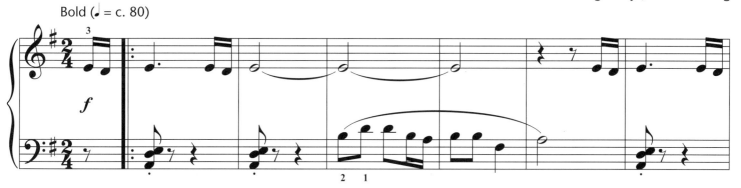

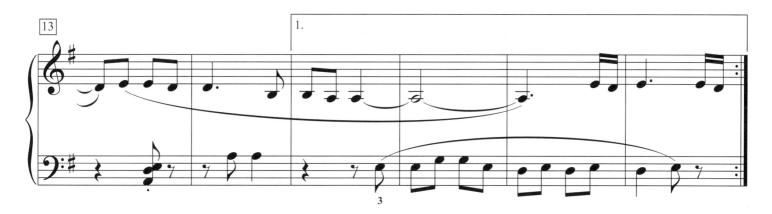

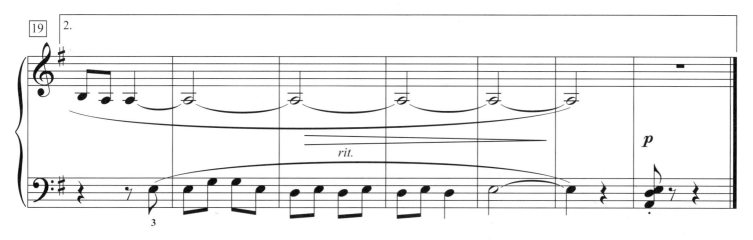

What Have We Done?
(Senzeni Na?)

South African Folk Song
Arranged by Nkululeko Zungu

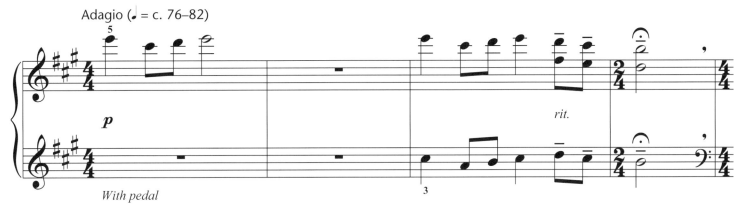

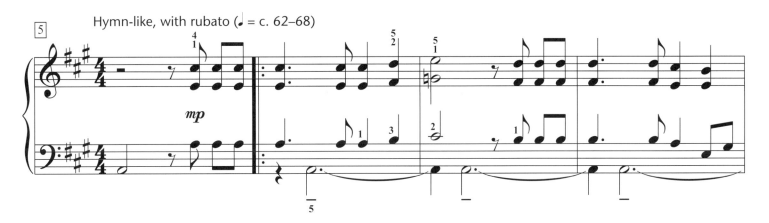

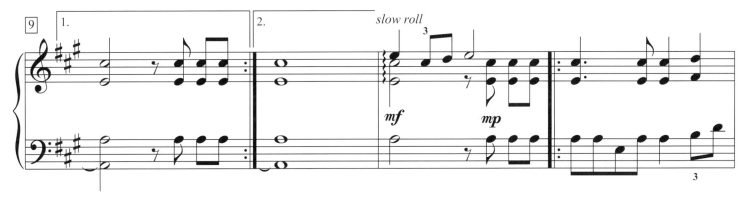

Hope, Don't Leave Me
(Thembekile)

South African Folk Song
Arranged by Nkululeko Zungu

At a walking pace (♩ = c. 100–110)

Light and playful

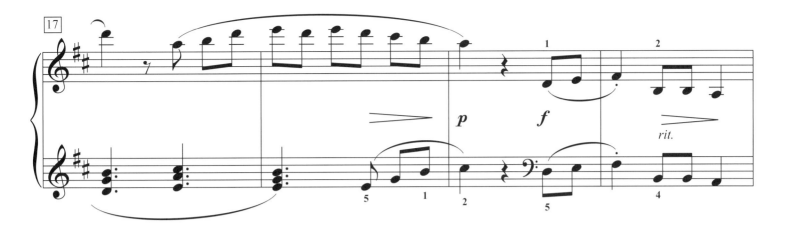

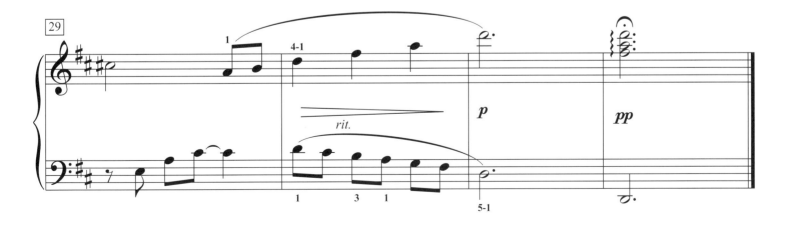

Delilah, My Wife, See My Strength
(Samson noDelilah)

South African Folk Song
Arranged by Nkululeko Zungu

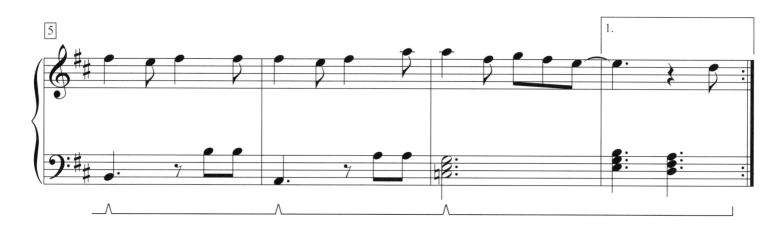

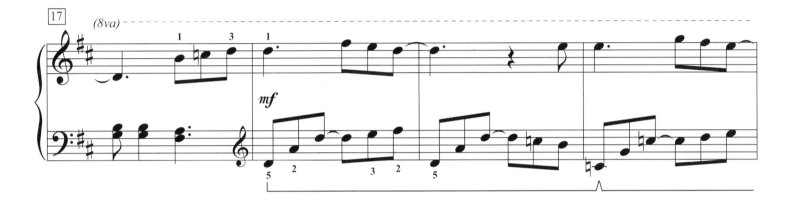

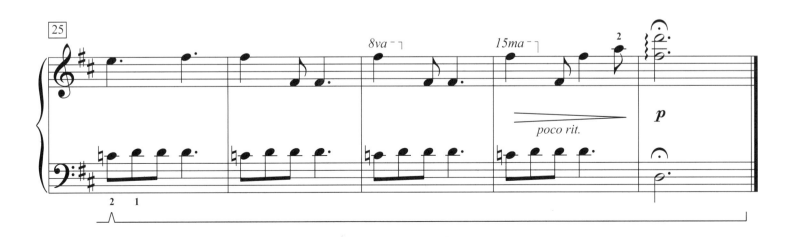

THE DOVES ABOVE
(NALO NALO NALO iHOBE)

South African Folk Song
Arranged by Nkululeko Zungu

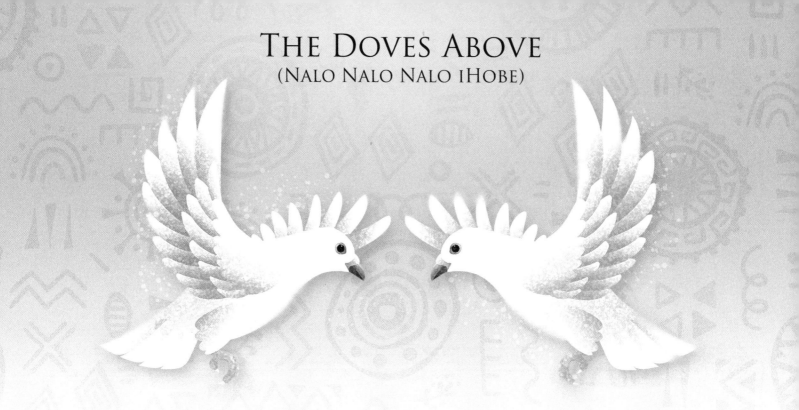

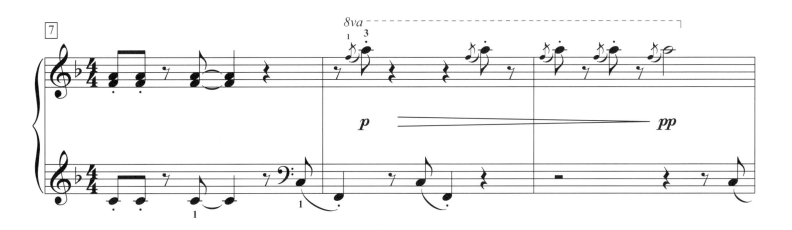

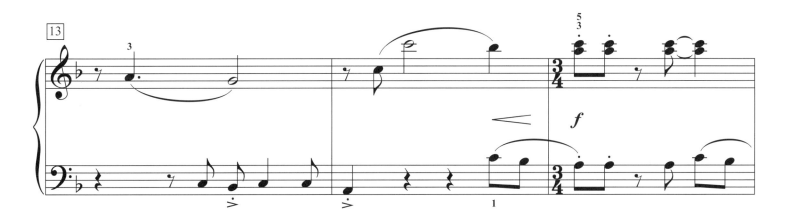

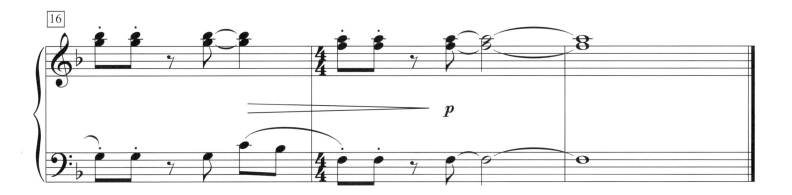

HERE COMES THE ALIBAMA
(DAAR KOM DIE ALIBAMA)

South African Folk Song
Arranged by James Wilding

Lively (♩ = 138)

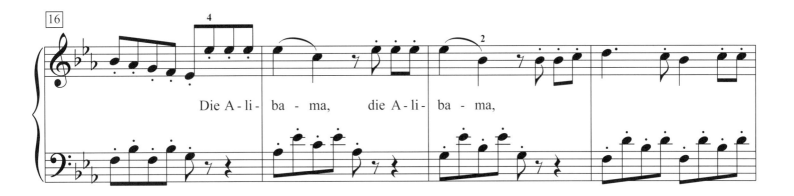

Die A - li- ba - ma, die A - li- ba - ma,

To Coda

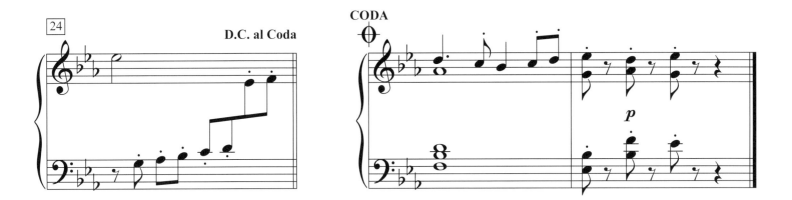

D.C. al Coda

CODA

p

Our Dearest Mothers
(OoMama Bethu, Esibathandayo)

South African Folk Song
Arranged by Nkululeko Zungu

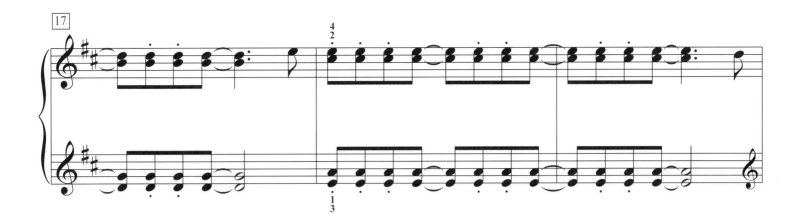

Sad and delicate (♩ = c. 92–98)

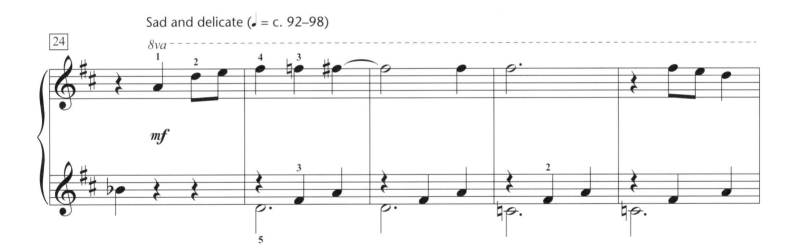

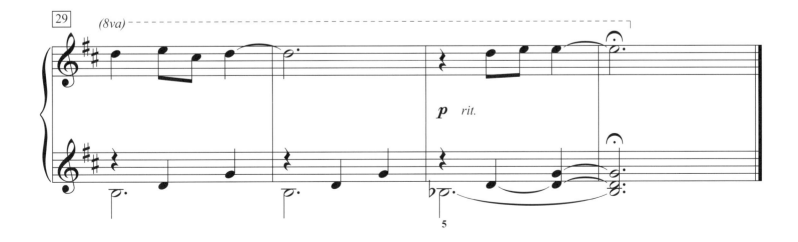

33

Sugar Bush
(Suikerbossie)

South African Folk Song
Arranged by James Wilding

Vivacious (♩ = 152)

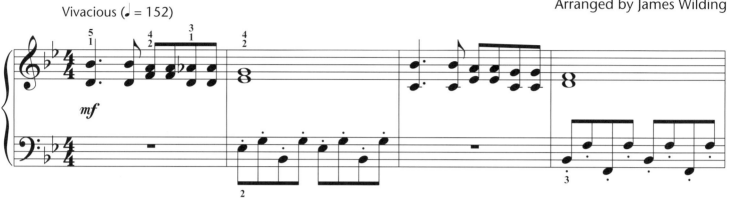

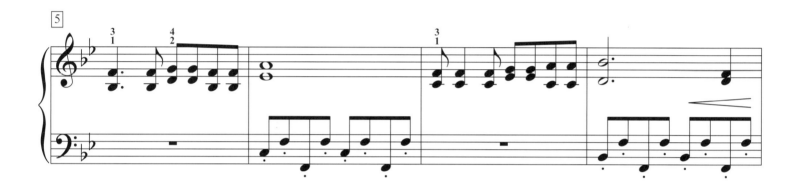

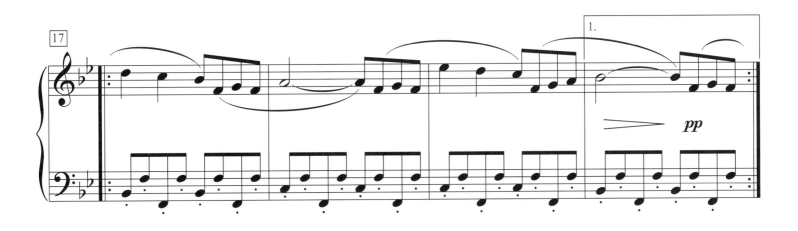

I Am in Charge, It Will Be Known
(Kuzakwaziwana)

South African Folk Song
Arranged by Nkululeko Zungu

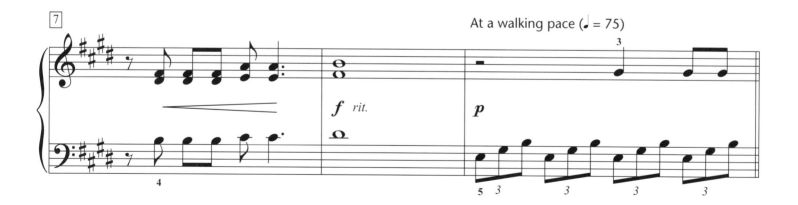

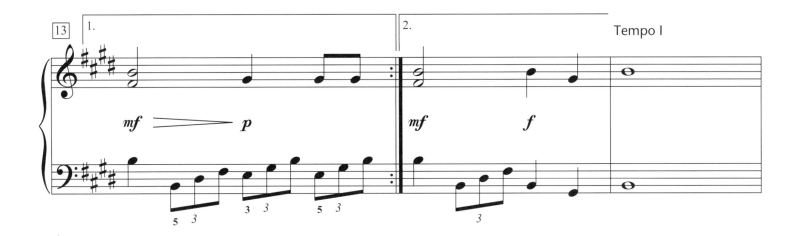

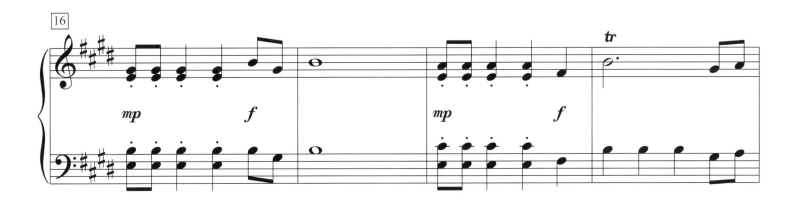

Go Forward
(Shosholoza)

South African Folk Song
Arranged by James Wilding

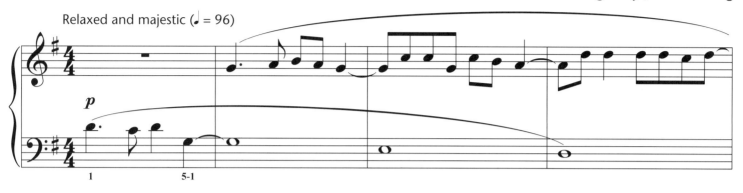

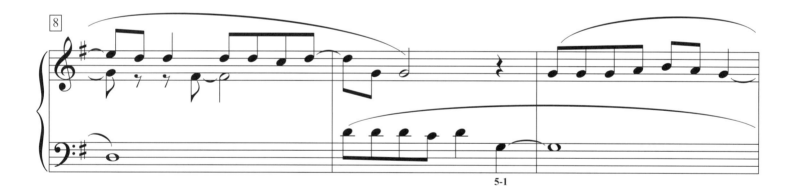

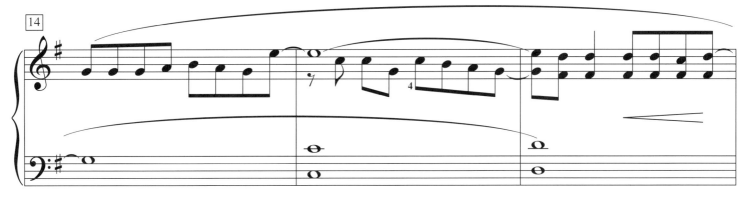

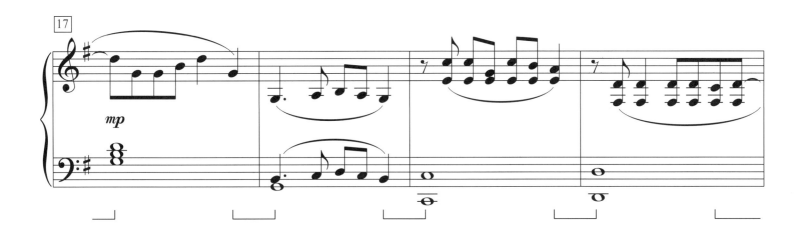

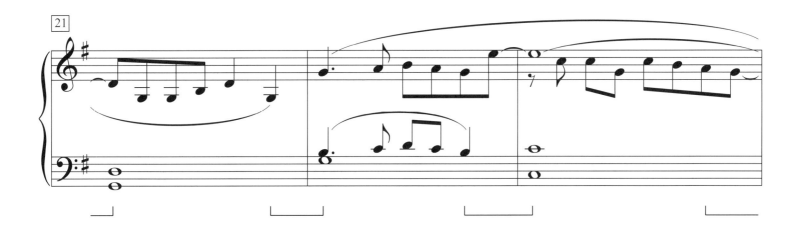

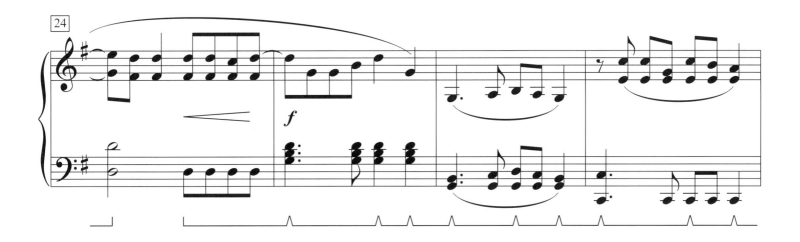

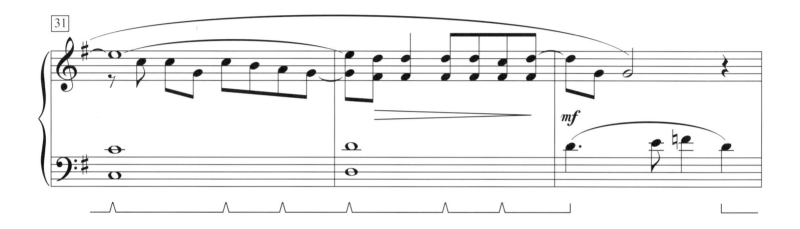

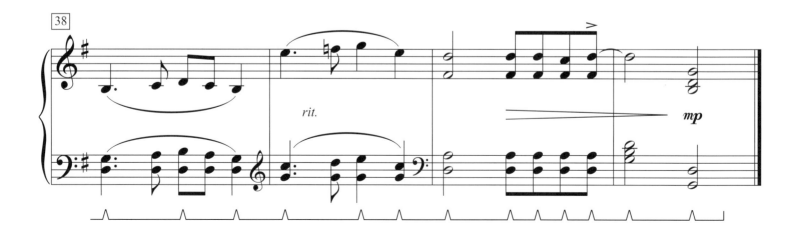

The Day We Pound Earth
(Motla Re Tulang Mobu)

South African Folk Song
Arranged by James Wilding

Spinning, like a wheel (♩ = c. 152)

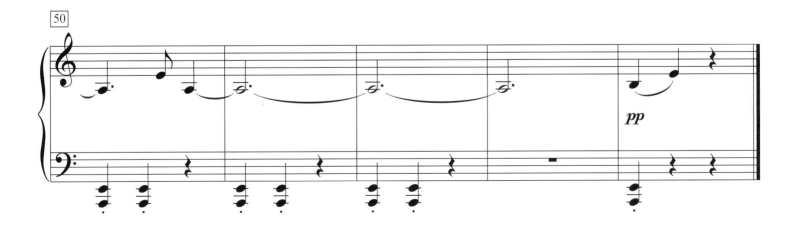

The Clouds, They Thunder
(Kwakhuphuka Amafu Dali, Leza Laduma Lamthata)

South African Folk Song
Arranged by Nkululeko Zungu

With unexpected drama (♩ = c. 110–120)

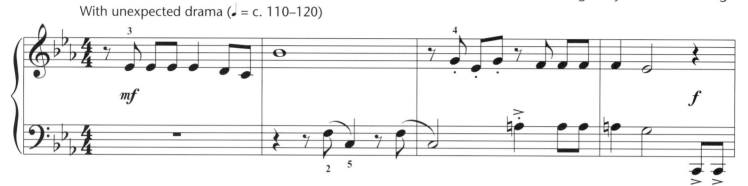

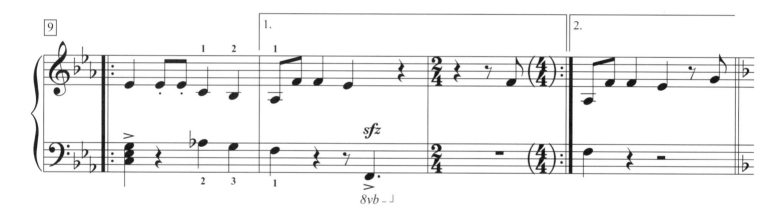

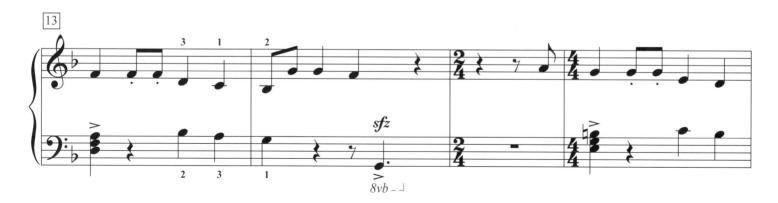

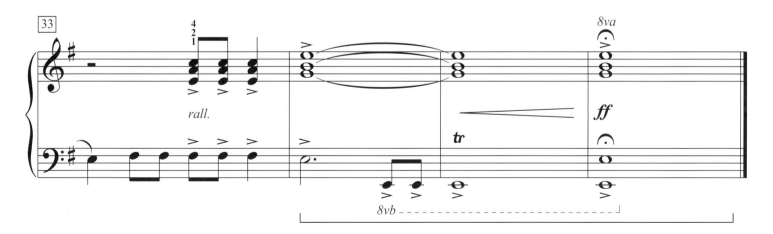

THE CROWING OF THE ROOSTER
(IQHUDE WEMA, LAKHALA KABINI KATHATHU)

South African Folk Song
Arranged by Nkululeko Zungu

Relaxed, with a lilt (♩ = c. 96–102)

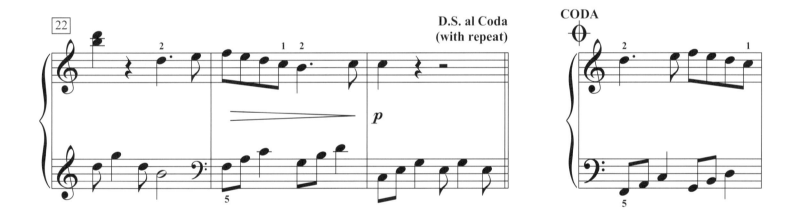

COME OUT OF YOUR CAVE, NCOFULA
(INCABA NO NCOFULA)

South African Folk Song
Arranged by James Wilding

Slow and mysterious, not in strict time (♩ = 72–80)
speeding up a little with crescendos and slowing back down with diminuendos

Bathed in pedal

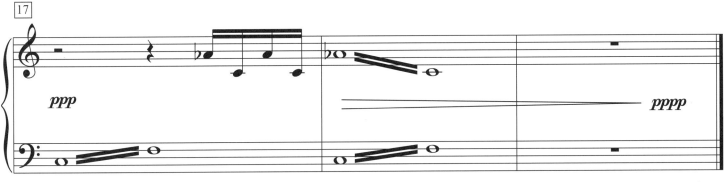

gradually lift the pedal —————————————————————————

HEY, THERE THEY ARE
(HEE KE BALE)

PERFORMANCE NOTES

- Play these six boxes in any order, starting wherever you like.
- When you finish a box, move right away to your next choice, without releasing the pedal.
- Each box should be played at least once.
- A box can be repeated whenever you wish.
- The piece ends when any box has been played three times.

South African Folk Song
Arranged by James Wilding

4.

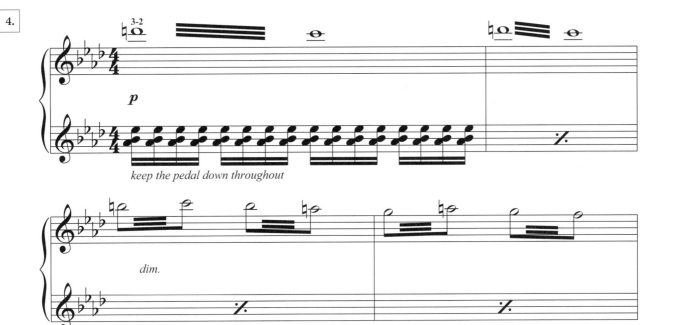

keep the pedal down throughout

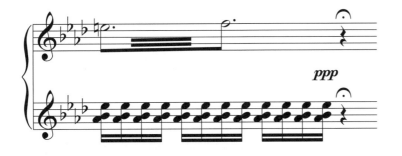

5.

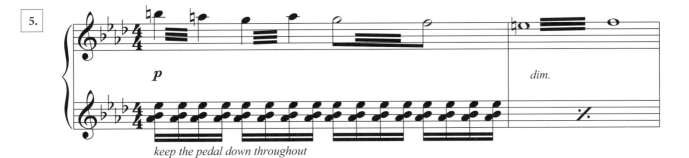

keep the pedal down throughout

6.

keep the pedal down throughout

DANCE
(MASESA)

Tap or speak this rhythm a few times before you start playing the piece

South African Folk Song
Arranged by James Wilding

Exciting and rhythmic (♪ = 208)

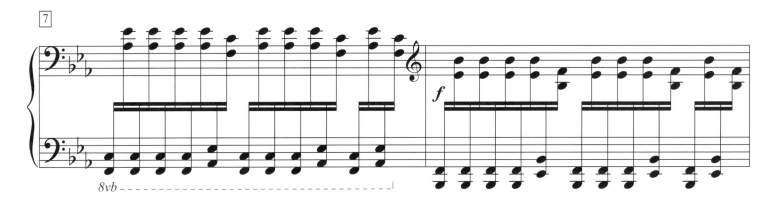

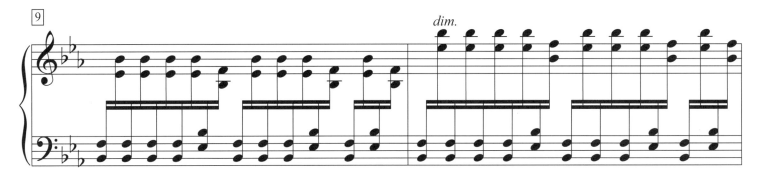

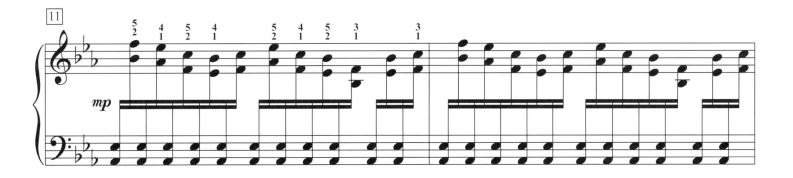

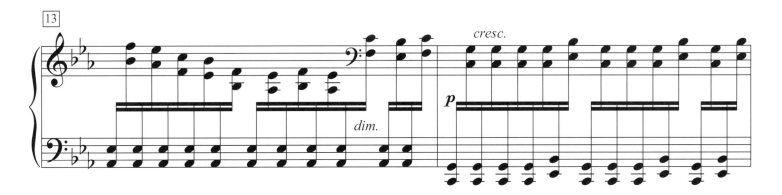

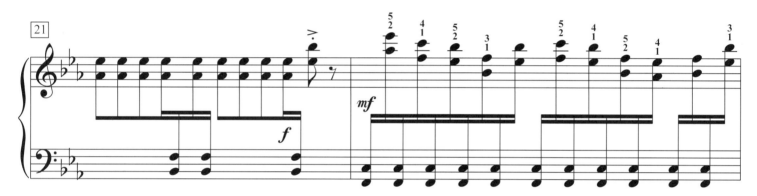

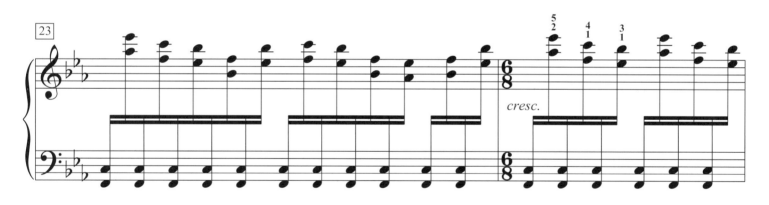

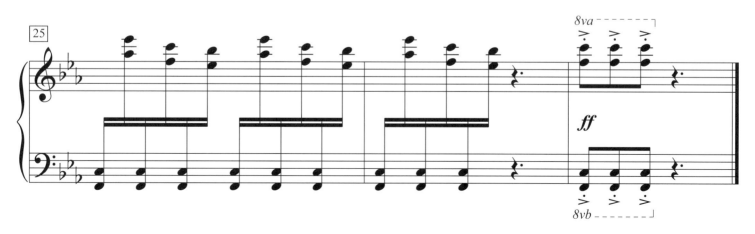

National Anthem of Lesotho

Lesotho fatshe la bontata rona,
Hara mafatshe le letle ke lona.
Ke moo re hlahileng,
Ke moo re holileng,
Rea le rata.

Molimo aku boloke Lesotho,
U felise lintoa le matshoenyeho.
Oho fatshe lena,
La bontata rona,
Le be le khotso.

TRANSLATION:

Lesotho, land of our Fathers,
You are the most beautiful country of all.
You give us birth,
In you we are reared
And you are dear to us.

Lord, we ask You to protect Lesotho.
Keep us free from conflict and tribulation
Oh, land of mine,
Land of our Fathers,
May you have peace.

LAND OF OUR FATHERS
(FATSHE LA BONTATA RONA)

National Anthem of Lesotho
Lyrics by Joshua Mohapeloa,
François Coillard and Adolphe Mabille
Music by Ferdinand Laur
Arranged by James Wilding

Slow and majestic (♩ = c. 63)

Variation I

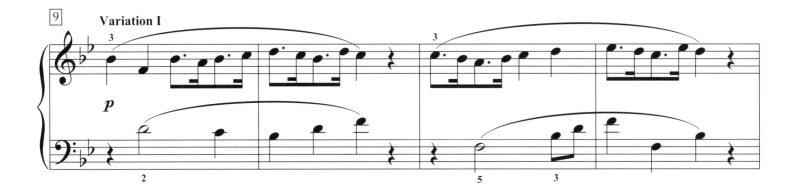

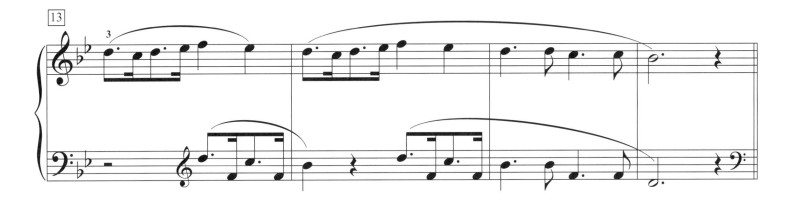

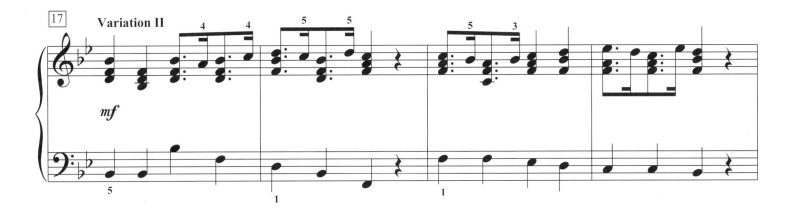

National Anthem of South Africa

(XHOSA)

Nkosi Sikelel' iAfrika
Maluphakanyisw' uphondo lwayo,

(ZULU)

Yizwa imithandazo yethu,
Nkosi sikelela, thina lusapho Iwayo.

(SESOTHO)

Morena boloka setjhaba sa heso,
O fedise dintwa le matshwenyeho,
O se boloke, O se boloke setjhaba sa heso,
Setjhaba sa, South Afrika, South Afrika.

(AFRIKAANS)

Uit die blou van onse hemel,
Uit die diepte van ons see,
Oor ons ewige gebergtes,
Waar die kranse antwoord gee.

(ENGLISH)

Sounds the call to come together,
And united we shall stand,
Let us live and strive for freedom,
In South Africa our land.

TRANSLATION OF FIRST 3 VERSES:

God bless Africa
May her glory be lifted high
Hear our prayers
God bless us, your children.

Lord, we ask You to protect our nation,
Intervene and end all conflicts,
Protect us, protect our nation,
Protect South Africa, South Africa.

From the blue of our skies,
From the depths of our seas,
Over our everlasting mountains,
Where the echoing crags resound.

God Bless Africa
(Nkosi Sikelel' iAfrika)

National Anthem of South Africa
Lyrics by Enoch Sontonga,
C.J. Langenhoven and Jeanne Zaidel-Rudolph
Music by Enoch Sontonga
and Marthinus Lourens de Villiers
Arranged by Nkululeko Zungu

Grand, with vigor (♩ = c. 100)

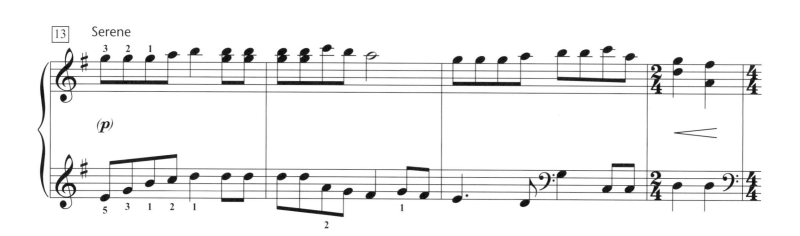

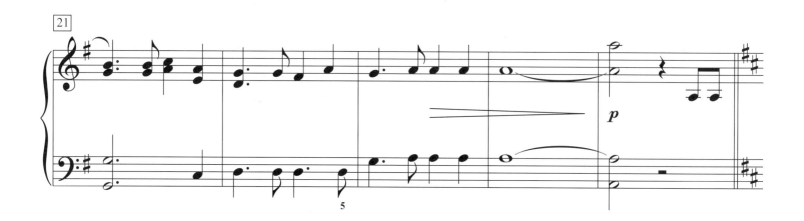

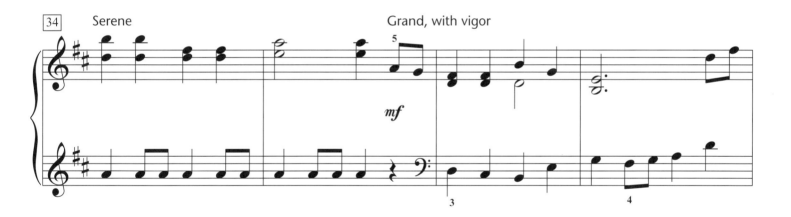

Guide to cultural groups, language, and traditions

AFRIKAANS (pronounced AH-FREE-KAHNS)

Originated in the 17th century when the Dutch East India Company decided to use the Cape as a midway point between Europe and Asia. Europeans gradually settled in the area and developed the language of Afrikaans.

AMANDEBELE (pronounced AH-MAH-NDEH-BEH-LEH)

Part of the Nguni people of Southern Africa. The language, isiNdebele, can be heard in the northern parts of South Africa and in neighboring Zimbabwe.

AMAXHOSA (pronounced AH-MAH-*KLOR-SAH)

The southernmost of the Nguni people. The language is isiXhosa. It is the second most spoken first language in South Africa and was Nelson Mandela's mother tongue.

> *The X here is an ejective voiceless alveo-lateral click, like the sound people in many cultures make when calling their pets!

AMAZULU (pronounced AH-MAH-ZOO-LOO)

The largest Nguni group and kingdom in Southern Africa. IsiZulu is the most widely spoken official language in South Africa and can be heard in KwaZulu-Natal and Gauteng.

BAPEDI (pronounced BAH-PEH-DEE)

Part of the North Sotho cultural group of Southern Africa. SePedi shares similarities with seTswana and seSotho and is spoken by many people in the Limpopo province.

BASOTHO (pronounced BAH-SOO-TOO)

A South Sotho cultural group between Lesotho and South Africa. The language, seSotho, is spoken from northwest to central South Africa and in neighboring countries like Namibia.

BATSWANA (pronounced BAH-TSWAH-NAH)

The BaTswana have been in the region since the 7th century and represent one of the oldest groups in South Africa. The language is seTswana, the primary language of the North West province and neighboring Botswana.

CAPE MALAY

Originated in the 17th century when the Dutch East India Company enslaved people from Southeast Asia and brought them to South Africa. The Cape Malay adopted Afrikaans as their language and developed it through interactions with other cultural groups to form their own unique variety, known as Kaap.

EMASWATI (pronounced EH-MAH-SWAH-TEE)

A distinctive Nguni culture between South Africa and the landlocked country of eSwatini (formerly known as Swaziland). The language spoken is siSwati.

VATSONGA (pronounced VAT-SONG-AH)

Another ethnic group made up of several subgroups, AmaShangaan being the most common. Their language, Xitsonga, is spoken in the Limpopo province and in neighboring Mozambique.

Map of South Africa and LeSotho

INDIAN
OCEAN

ATLANTIC
OCEAN

**SOUTH
AFRICA**

Gauteng
PEDI

Limpopo
TSONGA

Mpumalanga
SWAZI

North West
TSWANA

Free State
SOTHO

KwaZulu-Natal
ZULU

Northern Cape
AFRIKAANS

LESOTHO

Eastern Cape
XHOSA

Western Cape
MALAY

FOLK SONG COLLECTIONS
FOR PIANO SOLO

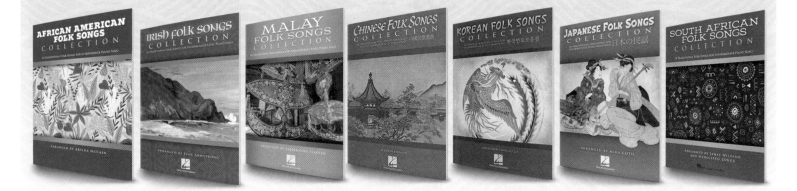

Introduce piano students to the music of world cultures with folk songs arranged for intermediate piano solo. Each collection features 24 folk songs and includes detailed notes about the folk songs, beautiful illustrations, as well as a map of the regions.

AFRICAN AMERICAN
arr. Artina McCain

The Bamboula • By and By • Deep River • Didn't My Lord Deliver Daniel? • Don't You Let Nobody Turn You Around • Every Time I Feel the Spirit • Give Me That Old Time Religion • Guide My Feet • I Want Jesus to Walk With Me • I Was Way Down A-Yonder • I'm a Soldier, Let Me Ride • In Bright Mansions Above • Lift Ev'ry Voice and Sing • Little David, Play on Your Harp • My Lord, What a Morning • Ride On, King Jesus • Run Mary Run • Sometimes I Feel Like a Motherless Child • Song of Conquest • Take Nabandji • Wade in the Water • Warriors' Song • Watch and Pray • What a Beautiful City.
00358084 Piano Solo...$12.99

IRISH
arr. June Armstrong

As I Walked Out One Morning • Ballinderry • Blind Mary • Bunclody • Carrickfergus • The Castle of Dromore (The October Winds) • The Cliffs of Doneen • The Coolin • Courtin' in the Kitchen • Down Among the Ditches O • Down by the Salley Gardens • The Fairy Woman of Lough Leane • Follow Me Up to Carlow • The Gartan Mother's Lullaby • Huish the Cat • I'll Tell My Ma • Kitty of Coleraine • The Londonderry Air • My Lagan Love • My Love Is an Arbutus • Rocky Road to Dublin • Slieve Gallion Braes • Squire Parsons • That Night in Bethlehem.
00234359 Piano Solo...$12.99

MALAY
(MALAYSIAN AND INDONESIAN)
arr. Charmaine Siagian

At Dawn • Chan Mali Chan • C'mon, Mama! • The Cockatoo • The Curvy Water Spinach Stalk • Five Little Chicks • God Bless the Sultan • The Goodbye Song • Great Indonesia • It's All Good Here • The Jumping Frog • Longing • Mak Inang • Milk Coffee • The Moon Kite • Morning Tide • My Country • Onward Singapore • Ponyfish • Song for the Ladybugs • The Stork Song • Suriram • Trek Tek Tek • Voyage of the Sampan.
00288420 Piano Solo...$10.99

CHINESE
arr. Joseph Johnson

Beating the Wild Hog • Blue Flower • Carrying Song • Crescent Moon • Darkening Sky • Digging for Potatoes • Girl's Lament • Great Wall • Hand Drum Song • Homesick • Jasmine Flower Song • Little Cowherd • Love Song of the Prarie • Memorial • Mountaintop View • Northwest Rains • Running Horse Mountain • Sad, Rainy Day • Song of the Clown • The Sun Came Up Happy • Wa-Ha-Ha • Wedding Veil • White Flower • Woven Basket.
00296764 Piano Solo..$12.99

KOREAN
arr. Lawrence Lee

Arirang • Autumn in the City • Birdie, Birdie • Boat Song • Catch the Tail • Chestnut • Cricket • Dance in the Moonlight • Five Hundred Years • Flowers • Fun Is Here • The Gate • Han River • Harvest • Jindo Field Song • Lullaby • The Mill • The Palace • The Pier • Three-Way Junction • Waterfall • Wild Herbs • Yearning • You and I.
00296810 Piano Solo...$12.99

JAPANESE
arr. Mika Goto

Blooming Flowers • Come Here, Fireflies • Counting Game • The Fisherman's Song • Going to the Shrine • Harvest Song • Itsuki Lullaby • Joyful Doll Festival • Kimigayo • Let's Sing • My Hometown • Picking Tea Leaves • The Rabbit on the Moon • Rain • Rain Showers • Rock-Paper-Scissors • Sakura • Seven Baby Crows • Takeda Lullaby • Time to Go Home • Village Festival • Where Are You From? • Wish I Could Go • You're It!
00296891 Piano Solo..$12.99

SOUTH AFRICAN
arr. James Wilding, Nkululeko Zungu

The Axe Cuts the Thorn Tree • The Clouds They Thunder •The Crowing of the Rooster • The Doves Above • God Bless Africa • Here Comes the Alibama • I Have a Sweetheart in Durban • Jan Pierewiet • Mama, Who Is This? • Our Dearest Mothers • Sarie Marais • Sugar Bush • They Say There's a Man in the Moon • What Have We Done? • and more!
00368666 Piano Solo $12.99

HAL•LEONARD®

halleonard.com

Prices, contents and availability subject to change without notice.